T0147912

Beyond The Realm

(Thoughts From Within)

by
Jude A. Brattoli

Order this book online at www.trafford.com
or email orders@trafford.com

Most Trafford titles are also available at major online book retailers.

© Copyright 2012 Jude A. Brattoli.
All rights reserved. No part of this publication may be reproduced, stored in a retrieval
system, or transmitted, in any form or by any means, electronic, mechanical, photocopying,
recording, or otherwise, without the written prior permission of the author.

Book cover photo and all photo illustrations were taken or produced by the author and/or
courtesy of the author's family.

Technical assistance provided by Dan Polovich.

Print information available on the last page.

ISBN: 978-1-4669-6837-0 (sc)
ISBN: 978-1-4669-6839-4 (hc)
ISBN: 978-1-4669-6838-7 (e)

Library of Congress Control Number: 2012921710

Trafford rev. 11/03/2015

 www.trafford.com

North America & international
toll-free: 1 888 232 4444 (USA & Canada)
fax: 812 355 4082

With love, to my family:

Each of you represents an individual, positive influence, within my life, that allows me the ability to express the emotions in my writings. While you may not have been aware of it, all of you have given me inspiration and added themes to my poetry.

Dad—Dedication and patience
Mom—Communication and counsel
Rita—Love of life and nature
Mark—Intellect and logic
Karen—Perseverance and determination
Mary—Compassion and trust
Jim—Philosophy and wisdom
John—Understanding and unconditional love
Bonnie—Beauty and spirit

I credit a time in life when family members joined together, as one unit, to share in all events, from meals to vacations, and from sadness to celebrations. I love you all.

Jude

Contents

Introduction

As human beings, we all possess an ability far greater than any other animal on Earth—the ability to reason and make decisions.

This being so, what makes each of us a unique individual? After all, a dog is a dog, a cat is a cat, and a bird is a bird. Along with other animal species, they all behave quite similar within their classification.

So again, what makes each of us so different? I say it is the power of emotion, our own interpretation of these feelings and how they affect us. To cite examples: Why do some people cry at weddings, or the birth of a baby? Why is it one person may find a roller coaster exhilarating, while another is too fearful to ride it? How can some people love a movie, while another group dislikes it? I cite these examples in the form of questions because you may have reasons that differ from that of another. Once again, it all lies within your own interpretation, powered by emotion.

In my previous book, *Moments In Time (A Collection of Expressions)* I gave no explanations of my poems, stating that the interpretations remain your own. I have, however, decided to break precedence by including a section, at the back of the book, with a brief description or insight as to the inspiration or theme behind a selection of the poems I have written. It is my attempt to offer the reader my view or explanation, which may very well differ from that of their own, thus proving the power of thought, expression, and emotion.

As before, I sincerely appreciate your interest in poetry and invite you on an adventure into the spirit of the soul. I only ask that you allow yourself to freely express your own emotions by thinking *Beyond The Realm.*

Jude A Brattoli

CHAPTER 1

Let's Talk

Too often we find that we're set in our mind,

Thus creating an altercation.

If I see things your way and you likewise, mine today,

Then we establish communication.

Speak No Evil

Ask me not of politics,

For I'll corrupt your mind,

But I'd gladly scratch your back

If you're willing to scratch mine.

Discuss not the sexes;

It is a battle without end.

If one finds himself outnumbered

There's no stand to defend.

If you speak of justice,

You may stand alone,

For I haven't enough money

To be the first to cast a stone.

Please, preach no religion

That you'd have me believe.

I can't add to its basket

When my hand's not received.

Healthy, Wealthy, And Weird

Red dye number five;

It's a wonder we're alive.

Don't smoke. Don't drink.

It's a wonder we can think.

Eggs and fat and bacon grease;

More bad things we must decrease.

Let's watch our weight and cholesterol.

You can take a pill for the rest of it all.

Insecticides and pesticides . . .

It's all a bit of suicide.

Smog, pollution, and acid rain . . .

We live in fear and live in vain.

Decaying birds and mosquito bites,

Allow billboards pop up overnight.

Radiation and microwaves . . .

By our own design, we are slaves.

Let's take a moment to catch our breath,

For we haven't lived, but accepted death.

A Friend In Need

What difference has changed your perception of me?

Would you stand bar against all I could be?

Would you steal my thunder, or shadow my dreams?

Would you cloud my visions with deceitful schemes?

Do you blow on the flame of my heart's desire

To let yours burn alone, brighter and higher?

Can you speak without guilt, your words of repression,

To dull my senses, like an act of aggression?

Deny me not life's quest to succeed;

For you measure by points, profits, and greed.

Don't pollute my ears with your talk about rules;

Lest we alter or bend them, we alone stand the fools.

So mute not my words and allow me speak free,

For together, one voice, perhaps we'll agree.

Don't misunderstand; there's no need to defend.

All that I ask is that you just be my friend.

The Counselor

Take to my shoulder when your head grows weary,

That the burden of your grief may rain upon me.

Be it my hand you grasp when you have fallen

And I will rescue your dignity from doubters.

Allow my eyes see what darkens the doors of your mind.

I will light the way and lead you to safe passage.

May my voice be the words you strain to speak.

I will herald the message and you shall be heard.

Give me authority to extinguish your anxiety

And allow my deeds defend your desires.

Trust and believe, that in the loyalty of your friendship,

Lies one who will guide, defend, and protect you.

For I am your shepherd, your strength, your shield.

I am the consigliore.

Love Always . . . Isn't All Ways

And the signature read, "Love Always."

But just yesterday, you took friendship away,

Yet the signature read, "Love Always."

I sat reading a note, from the past that you wrote,

And my mind wandered the path of our youth;

How we climbed apple trees, with bark skinned knees,

And sold lemonade from a cut up cardboard booth.

Whispered winds echoed childhood friends,

With secrets we promised in pact;

From faded years we grew, but still somehow I knew,

Our friendship, through change, was intact.

While thumbing a page, I awoke to my age,

And behind this child I no longer can hide;

But what words did I say, gave you right take away

The one true friend in whom I confide?

Thus, I struggle these words so frequently heard,

And we so freely write without thought;

So, if it's all just the same, I'll sign only my name,

As "Love Always," remains written for naught.

CHAPTER 2

Dream States

How mysterious be this state of mind,

In which the subconscious does subside.

Thoughts and deeds, in visions unwind,

And reality with fantasy collide.

Color Me Blue

I stand taller in blue,

With my shirt colored sky.

On my chest is a mirror of respect;

Its words reflect why.

There's a logo in thread sewn to my arm,

Cross-stitched in silk to protect it from harm.

A dark navy tie hangs round my neck.

I have a nine at my hip; I keep it in check.

I'm famous on stage, in red and blue lights,

Yet, I stand alone in darkness tonight.

I wear a dark hat on my head

To hide my deep thoughts,

But my eyes tell the story

Of a dream I have wrought.

Overlap

You returned yesterday, as though you had not a care;

My white rose of beauty, soft and fair.

We walked side by side; you and your game!

Teasing my love; have you no shame?

I walked you home, this white knight and his maiden.

I held back the wolves; kept you safe from the dragon.

You coaxed me draw near with a smile of grace.

To my arms you did fall in a lover's embrace.

A passionate desire burned like a fire in rage.

Dishonorable be a kiss, for I'm now twice your age.

Guilt overwhelmed me though I had you alone.

I belong to another and have a child of my own.

What cross-rip in time, or tunnel through space,

Has returned me here to this moment and place?

In a tumbler of glass sift the grains of sand;

You faded away and slipped through my hands.

The past and the present, in an electrical scheme,

Slumber in the mind and short circuit the dream.

R.O.T.U.M.

Beware! For you have not foreseen my warning.

Better for you that you grow ever conscious in

your mind and deeds, least you befall ill fated.

For I will find you, unsuspecting, in your weakest

sleeping hour, and like a plague, I will blacken your

world and take from you all you once held as sacred.

A darkness of evil will consume you, so great in power,

that you will cry out to be rescued, even upon Satan's wings.

I am not of his realm, nor yours. My presence possesses the

ability to pass through the corridors of all time and dimension;

fantasy and reality, memory and thought, emotion and spirit.

I am the energy of all that is unholy, the force of collective sin

from the beginning of time, and dark shadow to the secrets

of the eternal soul. I am the everlasting dream of torment.

I am Rotum.

Why?

Why is it emotions should run so deep?

Memory, like rain, pours down while I sleep.

Visions of you are the photos I keep.

Attraction, love, and lust intertwine.

Desire is the fruit that grows from its vines.

The taste on my lips from yours is like wine;

So why is it bitter, when recalled so kind?

Sweet passion be poison, in the guilt of my mind.

My conscience is the chains and the ropes that bind.

My spirit cries out; be steadfast and true!

But the suppression of honesty I can not do;

And why is it wrong, for me to love you?

Unsettled, I wrestle with commitment and faith;

But long last the night in fear of the wraith.

Instant Replay

Yesterday's voices and deeds unwind,

Over and over in the back of my mind.

The indecision of choices taps in my brain;

Like the storm out my window, down pours the rain.

Each flash of lightening is a fleeting thought.

Thunder echoes its replay in this game that I've wrought.

My past is a river and I trapped in its wake;

Memories flood in and the levee breaks.

Time lapse photos unfold like flowers.

Repeating snapshots fill restless hours.

My words return, to burn in my ears,

As recorded regret to capture my fears.

I request a time-out to post a yield,

But my subconscious controls the plays on the field.

Rewind, fast forward, pause, and play;

No stop, or eject with instant replay.

I'll Be Alright

Another night weeping in my sleep;
I awake cold and lonely in the deep.
But, you see, it's all these memories that I keep.
I see your smiling face above my bed
And gently draw my pillow to my head,
Trying to recall those words we said.

I'll be alright, if I can hold you tonight.
How real it did seem. All brought on by just a dream.
When the night time comes, I'm the lonely one, but
I'll be alright, if I could just hold you tonight.

I want to stay asleep for days.
Together, we could dream our love away.
Far from this world is where we'd stay.
These city streets are so unkind.
So many fools to love are blind,
But you're forever on my mind!

I'll be alright, if I can hold you tonight.
How real it did seem. All brought on by just a dream.
When the night time comes, I'm the lonely one, but
I'll be alright, if I could just hold you tonight.

I'll build a castle in the sand.
We'll walk the woods. I'll hold your hand.
Oh, why can't you understand?
Just a little longer, please!
Can't you see I'm on my knees?
But dreams have no sympathy . . .
You gently wave good-bye,
But the morning's not nearly nigh
And again, I break down and cry.

I'll be alright, if I can hold you tonight.
How real it did seem. All brought on by just a dream.
When the night time comes, I'm the lonely one, but
I'll be alright, if I could just hold you tonight.

CHAPTER 3

From the Heart

This beating muscle, within our chest,

Simply allows us to survive;

But the emotion attached, to this organ of life,

Lets us know that we're alive.

To You

To you, I would give my eyes.

Now behold what I see in you;

An angel in disguise.

To you, I would lend my heart.

Its warmth you feel is a kindled love

In a fire you did start.

To you, I would open my mind.

Reveal the thoughts I have of you;

Pleasant, gentle, and kind.

To you, I would expose my very soul.

Discover its secrets and share with me

All the love for you I hold.

Sleepless Love

Once more again, I could not find sleep.

You on my mind

In visions so kind;

I looked upon you while you slumbered deep.

Did I tell her today, "I love you, my dear?"

Did I hug her?

Did I kiss her?

Or allow her fall sleep after cross words I fear.

Know this my love, should you awake before me.

May the wings of a dove

Carry to you all my love

If my eyes shut tonight and never again do they see.

Love Trance

Mesmerized and hypnotized,

I'm paralyzed, when by your side.

I can't disguise this love that lies

Within my heart; I just can't hide.

I'm in distress, I must confess,

By the power you possess.

Your tenderness and sweet caress

Are like the spell of a sorceress.

You're a fragrant breeze that I must seize,

Like springtime blossoms, through the trees.

In your voice I freeze. Say something, please!

For you bring this grown man to his knees.

You hear my cries, but you don't realize

I'm trapped by the magic within your eyes.

The binds that tie are in your sighs.

Holding you does tranquilize.

To my heart it's love's lance. With you, I took chance.

Forever I'm a prisoner within your love trance.

Looking Glass Lie

Fair princess, she stands before her looking glass,

But only a faded, pale youth does she see.

No suitor comes call, or beckons her heart's release,

And thus, she waits anguished and betrayed.

Scornful words to herself she speaks,

Lamenting lost years of wasted love.

Her heart's true desire in passion burns,

And in the vile darkness, of an evil moon,

Again she cries out into a silencing night sky.

Oh, lonely maiden, turn away from this deceitful glass!

Its twisted image is but a false reflection of thee.

For I have beheld thy royal radiance of grace

And wish to rescue thee from this illusive plight.

Choose not the poison set there before you,

But run to tower's open window and call to me;

For I shall shatter this glass of foolish vanity

And forever free your heart from its prison.

A Winter Wish

I lie awake these lonely winter nights

Beneath a deep, dark, bitter blue.

There's the wanting warmth of a fireside,

And passion's fire that ignites with you.

It's your tender touch and candy kisses

That allow this man forget his woes.

So, I close my eyes and envision you,

But with empty arms, my heartache shows.

I recall your soothing, yet hushed lullaby;

In my ear, you'd softly sing.

Forever your voice, like the gentle rain,

From winter, you brought me spring.

Heaven's magic beams from your eyes,

So in their view I want to be.

There's a healing power in your fingertips;

One touch sets my spirit free.

I wish you here with whispered voice,

But like the silence of the night;

I'm left within the cold and dark,

Awaiting answer of your love's light.

Ever so quiet, I strain to hear

That reply return from you.

But in the waning hours of unrest,

There's only starlight's changing hue.

What change of fate will daylight bring?

Can winter winds whisk you here to me?

If I awake to find you by my side,

Is it dream desires that hold the key?

Sleep soon finds my weary eyes,

But before I drift away,

I call to you one last time

That your song might start my day.

A Distant Love

It was just yesterday when love came my way,

In soft words you said unto me.

Now I fear to go on, for that love may be gone.

Love that I was too blind to see.

If I could only change time, then you would be mine

And our love we could freely express.

Though fate's not on my side, still I can't hide,

A love that's so hard to repress.

If I could just find the way to stay here today,

I'd hold you forever, so fast.

But in life I have found, that faith holds us bound,

And I can not escape from my past.

But remember this, my love, when you hear the coo of a dove,

And look to a sky of pure blue.

Life may be just a game, but in my heart it's the same,

And it's all the love that I hold for you.

Love In The Air

My words recorded, await take flight,

While a crystal moon shines clear tonight.

It's my muse to you of song and dance;

A rhythmic beat that beckons romance.

I broadcast my thoughts against a velvet sky.

You need only listen; allow them amplify.

From the air to your ears, take into your heart,

This melody of magic that's pure from the start.

Transmit a signal so that I may believe,

You hear my love calling and wait to receive.

The music is soothing and the mood is just right.

Let's turn up the volume; we're in tune tonight.

It's an emotional balance of feelings begun.

Passion in stereo plays out as one.

So, fade to my arms and allow the frequency through.

I'm riding love's waves, from the heavens to you.

Mercy

I wasn't looking for the reality of a dream,
But then you wrapped your arms around me
And all those nights of sleepless searching,
Awoke me to the thought that it could be.

Yeah, that day I held your hand and kissed your lips;
But when your eyes pierced mine and you calmed my shake
I realized that far greater is love's magic, that
Too long I lay sleeping and was once again awake.

Can I hold on to this feeling? Oh God! Don't give up.
This school boy's just not up for the fight.
My cries echo out for mercy.
Can you hear them in the wind tonight?

Yes, I felt the tingles and the butterflies;
All the feelings a man would not admit.
But why should I deny all those charms
Given by my dream girl; given as a gift?

Tender and innocent was that moment
That I placed you high upon a shelf,
But in this jealous world
I know no other remedy, but to simply remove myself.

Can I hold on to this feeling? Oh God! Don't give up.
This school boy's just not up for the fight.
My cries echo out for mercy.
Can you hear them in the wind tonight?

CHAPTER 4

The Way Eye See It

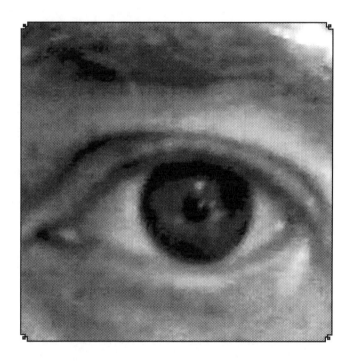

A magician's trick is nothing more

Than a simple slight of hand.

Look closer now, than you did before,

And perhaps you'll understand.

Stampede

From across the asphalt plains,

A rolling thunder echoes yesterday's cowboys.

Wild steeds, of iron and steel,

Snort the beat of a pounding stride.

I in my saddle, feet hard to the stirrups,

Clutch the leather reins and coax the mighty beast forward.

A hardened Stetson I don;

Its weathered, stiff brim shields my eyes

From these wilderness winds of strife.

To the front of the herd, without breaking her stride,

I watch for urban coyotes, but we continue the drive.

My horse does not weary, nor does she stray;

For we are one spirit; we ride in freedom today.

On Deck

A gentle breeze whispers a dead calm tonight.

From up on the deck, there's a view of heaven's starlight.

Floating lanterns, of yellow beacons that fly,

Signal a welcome as they flutter on by.

Mysterious black fiddles play out their tune

Like a rhythm of weather that's changing soon.

The moon, in its lighthouse, casts a shadow for me,

As I look cross the bow to a dark green sea.

No vampire pirates that would thirst tonight;

They'd meet their demise in humming neon light.

Though my ship rest anchored, in harbor this eve,

My thoughts have set sail and my spirit takes leave.

On board I am Captain, but many shipmates have I;

A company of dreamers beneath a starry sky.

Joyous revelry rings out as we raise our glass.

We toast to our freedom and the journeys of past.

Welcome aboard, should you wish join our clan.

Be one with us; a simple brotherhood of man.

Plea Of The Trees

Pale parchment, of a thousand trees,

Beckons I awake their legacy.

From Mother Earth untimely ripped,

Bartered, sold, and of beauty stripped.

Taken away in ropes and chains,

They cry to their brothers who stand in vain.

In an unfair trial, against their loss,

They're sentenced to be nailed upon the cross.

Some thrown to the fire, smothered by ash and soot;

Others are framed, or trampled under foot.

There's yet one fate, that does most disturb;

The ritual adorning and tossing to the curb.

So, the trees cry out their plea of duty,

"Restore our honor and our beauty."

Alas, poor me, I have failed that too;

I've written my words like a mock tattoo.

A Note To My Sun

My sun, where has thou traveled?

For in your absence, many a moment you've missed.

Your brother returned last eve, though weary from his flight.

I candidly remarked how his gray suit paled

In contrast to the bright attire in which you left.

Your sisters gathered round him upstairs,

Silently delighting in his company.

They dared not disturb Mother though,

For she was quietly resting below them.

Hectic was the day she spent running in circles,

So retired early after your departure.

Though your brother had not much to say,

We quietly strolled together along the garden.

I saw how he beamed over the flowers

That you and Mother had so carefully tended.

While your paths so seldom cross,

I wished that we all might be together,

Yet I know, upon your return, he will have departed.

The Winter Warlock

From within these cold walls, I sense Winter's dark heart.

Rapping and howling outside my doors and windows,

It wishes to trespass into the sanctity of my soul.

The metallic dragon snorts from the dungeon below,

Gnashing its teeth at this unwelcome predator.

Outside, soldiers of wood, stripped of their armor,

Stand frozen to the fury that will bend and break them.

From out of a purple haze, he leads his charge.

Riding a wild team of white horses,

He drives his front ever forward in blinding rage.

No mercy has he, in his siege against nature.

Trampling out the once vibrant colors of life,

He briskly sweeps through these sleepy streets,

Leaving a path of dust and drifting destruction.

From the hearth to the fire, I heat the steel of my sword;

Ready and armed to do battle with the Winter Warlock.

Stones

This stone from solid earth unloosed,

To roll and tumble through weeds and thorns.

Gathering no flowers, but shedding soil,

It weaves its path down a hillside green.

Sculpting a trail along its hurried journey,

It leaves a soft impression that others may follow.

With an indefinite direction of travel,

It continues to hurl toward its destination.

Faster the fury, increasing in speed,

It plunges to an awaiting pool of cleansing water.

With a shattering splash, into this new threshold,

It is sent to the silence of an unseen world;

But upon this new entry of rebirth,

It sends out a rippled tide of waves

That reach out and touch all the surrounding shores.

Life Cycles

The wind now marches east, bringing the cleansing rain.

Awaken fair colors from winter's death;

Spring forth and rejoice again.

Arise, dear sun. To thy children be fair and true.

I hear singing within your trees of green.

May vibrant flowers speak out their hues.

And thus, the season changes.

Mighty Helios thrusts down his bright swords.

Revelry I hear from the streets below

And parks fill with joyous hordes.

A celebration of fire rings out in a midnight sky;

Vows of honor, respect, and love exchange,

While summer sizzles by.

And again, the season changes.

Trees bow lower now as the sun takes daylight down.

Through this city the north winds stealth,

In the shapes of ghostly gowns.

Life's traffic light turns from green, to yellow—red.

Decaying colors on the ground,

Chant dirges for the dead.

Once more, the season changes.

The gray haired man now shuffles, in silence, through the night.

A painful gaze through frosted window,

I see vivid photos of black and white.

A bitter cold descends to hush this weary world;

Life, in cycles and seasons,

Through time and space is hurled.

Rap It Up

Check it out.

I'm gonna shout!

I've got a story and I gotta get the words out.

I'm not a rapper or a scrapper—

It's just a page, from my life, that ends another chapter.

I sit watchin, waitin, and just anticipatin.

Inspiration . . . the motivation

From the pen to this paper, it becomes my occupation.

The poet's curse . . . to write free verse

Make it terse . . . not reverse . . . even worse . . . call the nurse,

But I'm gonna write the words, till they take me in the hearse.

Can't understand this high demand,

But cursing in the lyrics gives ya more in da hand.

Damn it all! I'll take the fall!

What else can I do when I'm backed against the wall?

It's just so hard . . . the way things are . . .

Don't retard . . . take life's card . . . be on guard, and me disregard,

For these lines, I lament, are from just a lowly bard.

CHAPTER 5

Clouds

Within these dark days lies the troubled soul;

Burdened with worry, guilt, and control.

If one can see, beyond these black skies,

They know the sun shall return from behind its disguise.

Black Rain

Black rain—such pain—

A cloud of indelible stain.

Can't think—dry ink—

This quill in hand my bane.

Dark dreams—the rain teems—

A cold chill in my brain it seems.

How tragic—life's fabric,

Torn asunder at the seams.

Incomplete—a blank sheet,

To wrap me in defeat.

A phase—in one phrase—

A fate I can not cheat.

An empty zone—I am alone—

Carved in ice by a demon's hone.

Blinding glare—a blank stare—

I slowly turn to stone.

Lost grace—tears trace,

An older image in my face.

Can't write—a lost fight,

And a chapter I can't erase.

Untamed—a cruel game—

A sword to my soul to maim.

I've heard—one word;

Depression, the dragon's name.

A cage—pure rage—

A rapid decay of age.

So intense—my sentence;

It is master and I its lowly page.

Black rain, black rain;

I must endure its pain.

Black rain, black rain;

Once more, returns again.

The Temptress

Dark and mysterious,

A true goddess of deception;

But I see you hiding behind your innocence and youth.

Preying on emotions, to feast on affection,

You secretly conceal your seduction in silence.

I in my years, made wiser by time,

See through your disguise and this game that you play.

You, a delicate flower, in a fine china vase,

Hide your thorns of pain and heartbreak.

My beautiful rose, thou art truly captivating,

But your power grows weak by your needs

And the tending you require wears one weary.

Thus, I will continue to admire thee from afar.

I shall distance myself and stand ever guard

Against the temptress of my heart from whom I am barred.

The Note

No more to the steely knives shall I turn my back.

I am homeward bound and my bags are packed.

Rot well you vultures of lust and greed.

May you hunger and parish within your evil deeds.

Stand down oh you thieves that would prey on my soul;

My spirit lies bleeding in the heart that you stole.

I'll no longer bare witness to this pain and strife,

For I'm homeward bound to start a new life.

No more of these mysteries without single clues.

I've sang my last song and this trip's overdue.

So, I bid you farewell, with no remorse;

For the winds have changed and I must set my own course.

Dark Angel

Is life so dark that you can't think

Beyond the depths of Hell?

Awake, my dear, and see thy beauty

And allow it cast its spell.

For I see in you a gentle heart;

Not this deceiving role.

But I'll not subdue or cage your words,

For I know they're from the soul.

So pour forth and expel these demons

That would be your damning plight.

Cleanse thyself and be free.

Let your spirit take to flight.

(Dedicated to Jessica Galea, inspiring friend and fellow poet.)

Brain Storm

My thoughts adrift, I ponder my faded youth

And a time of tender, playful innocence.

A distant drum line, of a forthcoming storm,

Echoes back the lost laughter of my past.

Lightning flashes out still photos of black and white.

Snapshots from memory blink before my eyes

Then vanish within the recesses of a short, black calm.

A historic slide show, of moments in time,

Plays before me on the silver screen of a night sky.

Images pour forth, clouding my melancholy mind,

Till no more can I retain this coagulate collection.

The rain falls, as if to soak me in its solace;

But is this the rain of my redemption,

Or the mocking of these tears that I trace?

Hide And Seek

I wandered the path of my former youth,

But the wind had whisked clean these empty streets.

I searched for clues that time erased

And man buried beneath concrete.

Where was I then that I am not now?

And why be it so hard to find?

Could it be a flaw, within time and age,

That the child was left behind?

I stood waiting, as the light grew dim,

For a distant echo that might reply.

And the wise old trees, that stood there still,

Rustled to mock where that boy now lie.

I turned back slowly and through weary eyes,

I found that which I thought lost in vain.

For there in the light, of a pale moon,

Was the shadow of the child that remain.

The Cyclone

Within these gathering gray clouds of thought,

Lies the imbalance of my minds emotions.

Caught in a cross-rip of timeless memories,

I am drawn up into the cyclone's eye.

The gale force winds of change

Thrust me through the portal of life.

A clouded vision of innocence lost

Now lies in a dust covered past.

Spinning out of control, my eyes blurred,

I am blinded by a whirlwind of twisted emotions.

The soul fabric of my being is torn and uprooted

From the very foundation of my faith.

With no determined direction, downward I spiral,

Cutting a course of chaos and destruction.

Peering through a funnel of frustration,

I await the fate of my future.

Content I would be, in the comfort of the calm,

Had I only sought shelter from the storm.

The Empty Realm

Oh, from the melancholy mind of misfit toil,

Born is the demon of fraudulent spoils.

A misgiving to which he builds his kingdom;

Only to dwell in this fantasy freedom.

The delusions of grandeur, upon which he feeds,

Nourishes the evil of fruitless deeds.

Withered, diseased, and pestilence laden,

He takes the hand of the marquise maiden.

Together, they rule from an empty throne.

Behold the wickedness from madness grown.

Malice, deceit, and contempt as subjects,

They reign supreme over a shallow republic.

Within this desolate wasteland, of the blind,

Resides the tortured soul of the desperate mind.

Begotten from ill thoughts, that overwhelm,

Born is the child of the empty realm.

CHAPTER 6

Dedicated

This chapter is dedicated to the people

who have inspired, educated, and otherwise

made life, here on Earth, more meaningful.

Through their life's purpose, they have left

an impression that will forever last within

our hearts, dreams, desires, and our souls.

Ship Of Jules

It was a bitter, gray day when they brought her to port.

I recall how they gathered in show of support.

The crew had amassed to bid her farewell;

Stories they shared and of journeys did tell.

They painted and adorned her as one final duty;

Preserved for all to see her true beauty.

Their faces grew stern as they bowed in respect.

She had served them well, as the photos reflect.

With the sheets now drawn, no more would she sail.

The oarsmen assembled and took hold of the rail.

In procession they took her beyond the shore.

Now the vessel lay silent-to sail no more.

They placed her to rest by a marker of stone;

A lasting tribute inscribed-years of service shown.

As mates turned away, with tears in their eyes,

I felt no sadness, nor did I cry.

For within these waves of grief and strife,

She set sail once more with a new spirit of life.

(In loving memory of Julie Decker 1965-1996.

One of Earth's Angels)

Dear John

I can't imagine there's no countries

It's just so hard to do

All that we've fought and died for

Freedom and religion too

I see all the people

Praying for life in peace . . .

I can't imagine no possessions

It's a wonder that you can

In a world of greed and envy

It's in the nature of man

For I see all the people

Abusing all the world . . .

But yes, I am a dreamer

And I'm not the only one

Perhaps some day I'll join you

And we'll understand as one.

I do imagine there's a heaven

And here's my reason why

This earth be hell bellow us

Above us, polluted skies

I see all the people

Just trying to survive . . .

So yes, say I'm a dreamer

But I'm not the only one

A dreamer of peace one day was lost

When to Heaven, Earth delivered one.

(In fond memory of John Lennon, 1940-1980.

A man, that through his words and music,

dared us to think, 'Beyond The Realm.')

The Passage

I must leave you now, but cry not for me,

For I've flown beyond what thy eyes can see.

Though this vessel remain, here on earth,

I require it not within my soul's rebirth.

Although you grieve, take comfort my love;

For I'll guide and protect you from above.

Take solace in the words, "Thy will be done."

My spirit now flies with the rising sun.

Anguish not, of time lost with me;

By your side I'll always be.

From you I request but just one task;

This alone, is all I ask . . .

Take hands, embrace, and allow the healing start;

As I did for you, keep me in your heart.

(In loving memory of Sallyjane Munger 1938-2003.
Mother, sister, friend, caregiver . . . and my mother-in law.)

The Poe M

With never the chance of meeting, I informally formed a
greeting,
When unrest besieged my soul and upon my face did show.
Thus, I quoted, quill quickly in hand, "Shall I find words so
grand,
As that of just one man; the man, Edgar Allan Poe?
Alas," I lamented, "Never as grand as mister Poe—
                    Only he, and he I'll never know."

As I recall, twas late July, not night, but morning drawing nigh,
And I sat with great discomfort, beneath a humming neon glow.
My words strained to rhyme, under this dim light of lime,
As I begged borrow time; time with Edgar Allan Poe.
"Yes," thought I, "just a simple chat with mister Poe—
                    But no. For he, I'll never know."

Attempting once more to write, my eyes weary from pallid
light,
My spirit cried unto me, of an impending doom and woe.
"If I could just begin," to myself, said I again,
"To find prophetic words within, like Edgar Allan Poe.
Perhaps; if I could only share a moment with mister Poe—
                    Yet how? For he, I'll never know."

(Dedicated in memory and with the utmost respect, for a man
with incredible talent and vision. Edgar Allan Poe, 1809-1849)

Without A Trace

I gazed to the blackness of the night sky;

Like a shroud, it hides the truth.

Just as with the passing day,

My faith, like light, disappeared with youth.

How far off my thoughts did travel,

To a time when I shared life's joy.

Rain fell as tears upon my face;

I wept in silence-the abandoned boy.

It was you, who taught me the lust for life,

But something I can't comprehend;

You left so quickly when you had so much to give,

And alone, I'm now missing my friend.

You left me behind in your quest for all,

Just when I caught up to your pace.

I awoke one dawn and you were gone,

Leaving no footprints, or tracks to trace.

(In fond memory of my good friend, Daniel Dellman, 1951-2000)

The Sapling

Your words, like life giving water, rain down upon me.

I the seed, from the depths of darkness,

Shall emerge from this pod and take root

In the rich soil of your wisdom.

Springing forth from these earthly bonds,

I will grow and mature in the nurturing warmth of your friendship.

Teach me if you will, oh you trees of knowledge,

That the core of my heart may grow solid and strong.

Should we grow among weeds and thorns,

May the shade of our company allow them whither and rot,

Becoming fodder for fools and parasites.

The very grain of my being will be made smooth and sturdy

Within the shelter of our intertwined branches.

Alone, the strong, the weak, and even the poorest . . .

But united we stand, as the majestic forest.

(Dedicated to the members, friends, and family, of the
For the Love of Poetry Club, of N. Ridgeville Ohio,
for their infinite inspiration and support.)

CHAPTER 7

Lyf Is Short

Hold fast these moments we share today,

For tomorrow, they're but shadows of yesterday.

May they be solace and the lasting remedy,

Should we part one day leaving just memory.

Noon

If yesterday's tomorrow be but today,

Then what did light bring, when night faded away?

A tunnel of darkness with a light at its end;

From the center the same when we look back again.

An arc from this circle, a segment in time,

But you'll find there's no end, if you follow its line.

If the future's a moment, that's just up ahead;

Carpe diem the words, from the past we are led.

Time Clock

Life's mystic clock beats its drum,

With perfect rhythm, yet the tempo's numb.

No hands, no face, nor numbers show,

But time sweeps by and forward goes.

A moment now is but history.

Just a tick away, tomorrow be.

Within the power of time, days recede by hours;

Hours to minutes, we unfold like flowers.

The Scar

It is said that time heals all wounds.

What of this scar that still remains?

Left by you, with my heart in ruins;

Its reminder, to my soul, an everlasting pain.

But from within my heart, I forgive you now,

That inner peace may hide this mar;

For I know someday, somewhere, somehow,

You too, may suffer the scar.

A Fade In Time

That the hands of time should not stand still,

Watch the children grow.

For in the mirror, the image I'd will,

Was the child, from long ago.

Set Sail

Sunrise still brings yet another day,

Upon this orb on which we spin.

It is nothing more than a time delay,

That we might recant our sins.

So, let life be the sea that I sail.

I am captain of my own helm.

May my deeds be the winds that prevail

And mark course for that better realm.

Destination Unknown

Length, width, time and space;

A dimensional puzzle with science in place.

So much energy spent proving beliefs;

For an answer, a clue, or a bit of relief.

We see it and we feel it, therefore it is;

But is life not much more than a proverbial quiz?

Live, laugh, and love; let no time go to waste.

As for where we are headed, I'll leave it to faith.

CHAPTER 8

Above And Beyond

What lies beyond we hold in faith,

As we wander and we roam;

But when we see clear, our purpose here,

Then we'll find the path back home.

The Man In The Chair

An odd notion flowed through me, while on a retreat,

That someone was waiting, and I eager to meet.

As fate would grant it, as I walked through the door,

There was the man I met years before.

Though he remembered me not, by face or by name,

He was cheerful and helpful, and I intrigued just the same.

An insatiable thirst for knowledge filled the air.

Gathering courage, I questioned why he sits in the chair.

He gently smiled, caressing his cane,

"I'm not embarrassed to speak of my pain.

For you see before you an agnostic man,

But follow my story; perhaps you'll see as I can.

It was years ago that a vessel burst in my head;

Life's blood flowed out, leaving my right lobe dead.

I have no control of my left leg or arm,

Yet I sense the feeling of the cold and the warm."

I asked why the cane if he was unable to walk.

He stood, and he stepped, and continued to talk.

He explained his dance, while I in a stare,

And I watched him in awe as he returned to the chair.

I marveled his ability, though I was yet not aware,

Of the mystery behind the man in the chair.

For he told me of damage in the left lobe too,

And a tube from his brain, under his skin, shown through.

A clinical puzzle to doctors, amazed he's alive,

For what was left of his brain, barely let organs survive.

To his wife came the words of men in their greed;

"He will never survive and beds are in need."

She understood their dilemma, without reason to lie;

No one wanted to care for a man ready to die.

So she found him a place, quiet at best,

With wires and tubes; letting time do the rest.

I gazed more intently upon this agnostic man;

"Allow me finish my story. Perhaps you'll see as I can.

I slumbered five months, in a comatose state,

Then, like a rooster at dawn, I awoke, though quite late.

I was aware of my confinement, within hospital walls,

When a voice beckoned to me, but not from the halls.

I gazed to the bed, in this room two would share,

But I was alone. No one was there.

No doctors, no nurses, no medical staff;

I'm hearing things, I said. To myself, I did laugh.

Again, came the voice, calling to me;

Jerry, fear not, for I am here with thee.

My vision was clear and through my body warmth ran.

For there in my room stood, but a shadow of man.

He spoke of my struggle and this cross I must bare,

But he assured me of life and to trust in his care.

Now, you may not believe me, but I'm convinced it was real;

As sure as this chair," he said, his fist to the steel.

"Jerry, I believe you," I said, and extended my hand.

What passed in our grasp went beyond just the spirit of man.

(Inspired by the true story, as told to me, by Jerry Smith,
I met in Logan, Ohio, with my wife on our twentieth
wedding anniversary.)

Transparent

With a limited dimension, our eyes see what they can,

Thus you perceive me as just an image of man;

Not the true spirit or all that I am.

Flesh and bone, merely structure and frame,

A life force of blood, given a name;

And looking to you, I see but the same.

If I faded away and to the earth did return,

No more as this presence, then what would you learn?

Or be I just memory in the photo pages you turn?

You'll remember my deeds, my dreams, and you'll find,

Family and friendships, and loves left behind;

But can you see even deeper and open your mind?

For there's a spirit of being, beyond life's stage,

Of a dimensional battle, in our mind that we wage;

And it's the realm of the soul; still a mystery of age.

Stone Cold Visit

Driving by the other day,

I think I'll stop; maybe stay.

It's been a while at least for me.

You were solemn, but had reason be.

I'd been away too long and you knew why,

For you watched me almost pass you by.

You were difficult to find for things had changed.

Weeds had grown high with floral colors rearranged.

Perhaps you needed help with some tending,

So I quietly went about doing mending.

I took to chatting while about my task;

You said nothing, nor a question ask.

I remarked of this gentle, sun lit day.

You remained silent, with nothing to say.

Remorse filled my heart. Forgive me, please.

I began to cry and fell to my knees.

But I'll not forget, as I said good-bye,

The golden Monarch that fluttered by.

Beyond The Senses

Seek and thee shall find,

But search not with your eyes,

For in their weakness thou art blind,

And true desire slumbers in the mind.

Knock and the door shall be open to you,

But expect no greeting of extended hand,

For this threshold of life is but for the few,

And by deeds of the heart that you pass through.

Ask and thou shall receive and be made whole,

But wait not for something to grasp in hand,

For the riches and treasures, that would be your goal,

Lie beyond this realm and within the soul.

Connect The Dots

In a majestic night sky the stars connect.

By day, jet stream clouds that intersect.

Waves of power lines strung post to post;

Electric life travels coast to coast.

Drops of rain once set in motion,

Led by the stream, become the ocean.

The silk of the shore, upon which I stand,

Is nothing more than threads of sand.

From the mountain tops to the circling seas,

The eagle takes flight on a misty breeze.

Outstretched cables, supporting the bridge,

Allow us pass safely across a dangerous ridge.

So I've come to ponder, faith, hope, and love,

Charity, forgiveness, and heaven above.

To which of these roads should we respond?

That will take us from today to the realm beyond.

Hunters In The Haze

An early morning fog, rising up from a sleepy valley, lay reminder to this late autumn rainfall. Stepping out of a cozy, quaint chalet, to which I retreated, my face is greeted by a brisk December numb. An aromatic vapor of rich coffee whisks up from my cup; my hands gently caressing its warm ceramic to pull the chill from my fingertips. Tiny pellets of ice lined the deck rail, sparkling like small diamond chips. Though the Birch, Oaks, and Maples lay barren of color, there still remains the deep green foliage of Cinnamon and Christmas ferns, growing among the Virginia pines. Raising my wrist, I rub the watch dial face of its daybreak dew. As if to toll the hour, a single shotgun blast rings out and fades in echo through the rolling hills. Somewhere in the distance, a hunter's gun releases a quick plume of gray smoke. His breath relaxed, emits a resounding reply to the heated steel muzzle. On the forest floor lies a fallen life force; its spirit given up in a cloud of warm blood steam that rises to greet the morning mist. A momentary silence brings the revelation: I too, like the hunter, huddled in the haze, had found that which I had sought.

Full Circle

I awoke one night with troubled mind

And upon life's riddle I did ponder.

I recalled the words of seek and find,

So decided thus to wander.

I went to the house of brick and stone,

Where stain glass towered to the ceiling.

Turning round, I now stood alone,

In a man built room that gave no healing.

I ventured up to the mountain's crest

And toward the heavens I did gaze.

A pair of eagles did fly abreast,

Yet my spirit did not raise.

I journeyed out to the ocean's shore;

Its splendor was beyond compare.

White foam waves crashed and roared,

But the answer was not there.

I retreated within a forest view

Of mighty Redwoods, Oaks, and Pines.

Nature's life in cycles grew

And I took solace in its shrine.

Empty handed, I returned back home,

While still questioning my faith.

Shall I be forced to forever roam?

Will I fall prey to a demon wraith?

I turned to the book of spoken word,

Determined to ease my mind,

And there on a page, read those words;

Seek, and thee shall find.

Restless, I retired once more,

Yet still, I pondered why?

Then came the thought, I had not before,

Perhaps the answer is truly I.

A Test Of Faith

How many times must a man falter

Before he reach his goal?

How many sins can he keep within

Till alas, he lose his soul?

No answers have I, but I'll not deny,

It is all in his control.

So, call to your gods, your idols of stone;

The stars, the moon, and the sun.

I'll not cast the first stone, for I stand here alone,

And there's no number greater than One.

The Abyss

That which I can not see is the basis of what I seek.

That which I can not touch has become my desire to attain;

And what it is that I wish to possess is the object of my quest.

Between the mysteries of the mind and the emotion of the heart,

There lies the abyss—the portal to the secrets of the soul.

Extract this hidden organ that I may examine its contents.

Allow me access to its operational functions of life,

So that I may come to understand the purpose for which it exists.

But no . . . no scalpel can cut it; no instrument shall ever reach it,

And no human hand shall ever touch it.

So, where does it lie? Why do I not feel the physical,

Yet I sense the power of this invisible, driving force?

Within this duality rests all that I hold in trust:

Beauty and love, honor and respect, and compassion and wisdom.

All this, and more, has become the morality upon

which I base my search.

Yet it is on faith alone that I go blindly and deeper into the abyss.

Changing Tides

A spinning wheel of blue and green,

Speckled red and gold psychedelic dots;

Reminds me of a time I long for . . .

That with time, time itself forgot.

I see children holding infants,

Yet they not fully grown.

Who now guides these pair of babes,

As they seek out on their own?

A child cradled in a manger

Born that he might save this world;

So far we've come, and so much undone,

And yet farther away are we thus hurled.

CHAPTER 9

Encore

Life is a stage and we all play a part.

The role may be large or quite small.

If you take your role and act from the heart,

They'll cry for more at the end of it all.

Ashes to Ashes

What man lie trapped behind the eyes

Of the one that leads him?

Within the shadow of he who walks upright,

Sleeps the spirit of truth.

Be not deceived by this mirror of flesh—

An infinite image reflected back again.

This parlor trick, of timeless age, holds no answer.

Through birth he inhales the soul.

Held in check by the body, guided by the mind,

And consoled in faith, he expels its worth with his last breath.

From out of ashes is born a man of earth

And to the soil, from which he came, he shall return.

Voodoo

Needles and pins run under my skin.

It's an ancient black magic—an angel's sin.

My blood runs hot then flows cold as ice.

I'm bound and held captive by a sorceress device.

Just a rag doll placed in a cardboard box

With a bleeding heart and fresh cut locks.

Like a knife to my chest, it's a mortal pain,

But fighting its spell is an attempt made in vain.

One candle burns brighter, within a ring of fire,

To ignite the theme of one night's desire.

A puppet on wires, to dance and sing—

Controlled by the hand that pulls the strings.

It's the master's hand that now holds my fate,

For in the bewitching hour redemption's too late.

The Reception

Distant shadows of memories forgotten

Now steal the tranquil blue spotlight of a midnight moon.

They bid me take dance; provocatively pleading I take their hand.

An illicit affair of time and thought, I dare not fall slumber.

Still, fancy are these psychedelic colors that besiege my nights.

Voices of the past travel a timeless wave and hauntingly return

On an echoed wind, through hollow branches.

Restless spirits that linger in the recesses of my mind,

Still seek out the one who will cater to their hunger.

In repetitive fashion, I must now entertain my guests.

They will feast upon my intellect and drink up my soul.

Friends, foes, and lovers; all in glad attire,

Eagerly await my attention in the reception line.

Raspberries

Raspberries,

Fresh, pungent raspberries.

The smell still lingers sweet on my pillow.

But not there, no; it was early morn.

I plucked that scent from a fresh garden harvest.

Timing so perfect that the odor would last me all day

And that I should nod off to sleep

With the fragrance as ripe as the vine

That waits yet another tasting of its fruit.

Beautiful Thorns

Behold the rose in beauty splendor;

Its petals of silk are soft and tender.

Awoken by Spring, it blossom and flourish.

To the nose of the romantic, it's a scent to nourish.

Written as love by the poet's hand,

To caress his words and give them command.

Watch it grow tall in the summer sun.

It's given from the heart to my true one.

Beware the thorns that course its veins.

Love comes at a cost. To some it pains.

Through Child Eyes

I once gazed upon her innocence, with a heart felt, gentle sigh;

From a child's undaunted world, came the questions,

"Daddy . . . why?"

My answers returned quite swiftly, in soft words she'd understand;

What a simple miracle—a child's smile, and her hand

within my hand.

I'd often take a knee, that I might see her world's view,

And within her eyes I saw what I already knew.

The inquisitive mind of youth can be such a joyful pleasure,

But, to be the center of their truth is a grace you can not measure.

Now the years have faded by and within the setting of the sun;

The child became a woman and thus the teacher's job is done.

So, now you realize the power that led me through,

But can you sense my pain, for I've nothing left to do.

It is now that my soul is troubled, as I gaze to a midnight sky,

And through the eyes of a child I ask the question,

"Father . . . why?"

Safe Harbor

Somber winds, in a twilight hour, return the fragrance of my youth.

There sits that child still, with textbook—blind and mute.

A scent of lilacs whispered though an open window, into that room;

Whisking me away to a time and place where a boy's

imagination reigned supreme.

Away from those red bricks of confinement and silent stone—

On a carpet breeze I rode to the land of evermore.

The sun drenched teacups of the daffodils gave early signal

To the vibrant forthcoming of summer and

freedom from responsibility.

Within the arms of the oaks, cedars and maples,

I would build my refuge and parley with the face of age.

I adorned myself in the spoils of richly earth and an azure sky.

I danced with Mother Nature.

I softly kissed the cheek of lady innocence.

Untold secrets lie there still, buried among the rocks

and reeds of a quiet stream.

Like a pirate at sea, this time was mine to pillage.

Better than truth, save the fact, my dreams were of solid gold.

Author's Explanation of Poems

Speak No Evil—A personal view, or opinion, on the subjects of politics, sex, and religion. Three topics of discussion, we often view as taboo.

Overlap—Author's dream of a teenage 'crush.' In this dream I am of current age, while my would be love, events, and surroundings were that of past age and memory.

R.O.T.U.M.—Only a small hint of this nightmare, here. Realm Of The Unconscious Mind.

Stampede—A metaphoric expression for the author's enjoyment of motorcycling. ". . . asphalt plains . . ." represents the roadway. "Wild steeds of iron and steel . . ." are the motorcycles. ". . . urban coyotes . . ." is the surrounding traffic.

Looking Glass Lie—Inspired in part by the many stories of love, fantasy, and fairytales, such as Romeo and Juliet, Cinderella, Snow White, etc. I find a common theme of a lonely, but beautiful maiden, who desires the love of just one man to come to her heart's rescue. Her fear of rejection often becomes her own inadequacy to realize her own true beauty and the possibility of multiple suitors, who desire her as well.

Stones—In life, we pass through stages of dependency, independency, and interdependency. "This stone from solid earth unloosed . . ." is representative of our birth, while ". . . weeds and thorns." are the obstacles or challenges we face as we mature to the stage of independency. ". . . soft impression that others may follow." is that part of life in which we lead by example, through career choices, parenting, or teaching others. Interdependency is the giving of ourselves, back to the community, that others may benefit from our life's knowledge or experiences, thus . . . "It sends out a rippled tide of waves . . ."